Check, Check, SOLD

*A Checklist Guide To Selling Your Home
For More Money Without an Agent*

By

Jake Posey

Edited By

Beth Whittaker

DEDICATION

To my awesome wife, Amy, who enables me to follow my dreams.

BRAND NEW BONUS...AVAILABLE FOR THE FIRST TIME

I am so excited to announce a brand new bonus that was just added for this book. For the first time, I am giving you access to my Home Selling Academy for FREE.

Yep, that is right. It is 100% free.

This is the same course that I priced at $49. Jump to the end of the book to learn how you can get access to this course today (I had to put it at the end of the book to limit access to people who bought the book).

Why am I giving you this for free? The answer is simple...I want to put real estate agents out of business :-)

BONUS MATERIALS

Throughout this book, you will see references to worksheets, videos and interviews that are available from the FSBO Academy. These bonuses are available for free at www.fsboacademy.com/freebookbonus.

CONTENTS

ACKNOWLEDGMENTS

I want to give a special thank you to my mother who trusted me to help her sell her house without an agent. I also want to thank my wife Amy and daughter Caroline for putting up with me while I locked myself in my office conducting interviews and writing and rewriting this book. I want to thank my assistant Hope Laniojan, for helping me organize all of my ideas and publishing this book. I want to thank my editor, Beth Whittaker, for her tireless effort in making me sound intelligent and helping you understand my ideas. Finally, I want to thank all of the homeowners and professionals I interviewed for providing all the content that went into this book.

CHAPTER 1:
PROCESS OVERVIEW

Selling your house on your own is not that much different than selling your house with a Real Estate Agent. The main difference is that instead of giving information to your Real Estate Agent, you are entering this information into web forms yourself. You are also making and returning phone calls yourself.

Selling your house can be an overwhelming process on its own, regardless of whether you are using an agent or not. When it comes down to it though, selling on your own in not that much more work.

Here is an overview of the process at a very high level. I will get into some additional detail in the sections to follow. Note that the items in bold are things you need to do on your own when you kick the Real Estate Agent to the curb.

1. Decide to sell your house.
2. Hire a Real Estate Attorney.
3. **Determine the price for which you will list your house.**
4. Get your house ready for sale, both inside and outside.
5. Take pictures of your house.
6. **List your house for sale online and place a sign in the yard.**
7. **Show your house to interested, approved buyers.**
8. **If things are slow...**
    a. **Hold an open house.**
    b. **List your house on the MLS system.**
9. Negotiate an offer with a buyer.
10. Accept your offer and sign the sales contract.
11. Provide access to your house for the buyer's "people."

12.   Check in on the closing process.
13.   Attend the closing and sign the paperwork.
14.   Deposit your check.

If you ever get depressed and are tempted to call an agent to sell your house, remember 2 things.

1.   You have already done all the hard work; you just have to be patient now.
2.   Every single seller I interviewed who has sold at least one house on their own says that they will never go back to using an Agent again. That is 100% satisfaction!

CHAPTER 2:
HIRING A REAL ESTATE ATTORNEY

Hiring a Real Estate Attorney is the most important part of selling your house on your own. Once you have your Real Estate Attorney, he or she will guide you through the process and make sure you do everything right. Here is your checklist on hiring a Real Estate Attorney.

Finding the Right Real Estate Attorney

Referrals are the best. Post this message on the social media sites you use. "Does anyone know a good Real Estate Attorney?"

If you don't get any referrals, search online at...

Martindale – www.martindale.com/Find-Lawyers-and-Law-Firms.aspx
This website allows you to search by area of expertise and lets you know if the attorney has been reviewed by his/her peers and by clients. It gives you an aggregate of the reviews, but does not show individual reviews.

Avvo – http://www.avvo.com/
This site lets you post free questions to attorneys and find local attorneys by specialty. You can view internet reviews on the attorneys as well.

Introduction Script

Once you have a few Attorneys in mind, it is time to call them and ask a few questions. Here is a script to use.

"Hi my name is _____, and I live in _____. I was recommended to you by _____ (tell them if it was a website too). I am getting ready to sell my house without a Real Estate Agent. I am looking for a Real Estate Attorney. Do you have 15 non-billable minutes to answer some questions to help me determine who to hire?"

This short intro gives the attorney a lot of information about you. It provides information on your location, so the attorney can immediately assess if he/she can help you. It also conveys how you found the attorney, which is helpful for his/her advertising purposes. Finally, this lets the attorney know that you are shopping around and this conversation is not billable.

Questions to Ask

☐ **Can you explain the Real Estate process to me and the assistance you will provide at each stage?** You want an attorney that can simplify things and explain them in terms you can understand. If you feel overwhelmed or confused after this question, you should say, "Thank you for your time, good bye." The real estate sale process seems complicated, when it fact, it is really easy. If someone makes it sound complicated, that is a red flag.

☐ **Can you walk me through the list of services you will likely provide me and the price for each service? Also, make sure to tell me when I will be billed for each service?** When this question is answered, ask if the attorney could email the information to you as well. This question will help you understand where your money is going and when you will have to write a check. Expect most, if not all the fees to be paid at closing.

☐ **Do I need to hire a title company if I hire you?** Some attorneys are Title Agents and can provide the title services and insurance, while others are not. Ideally you want an attorney who can handle everything.

☐ **If yes, do you have 2-3 title companies that you would recommend?** You want to ask for multiple companies for two reasons. First, if the same title company names keep coming up as you are talking to different attorneys, this is a sign they are good. Secondly, good attorneys grow their business by helping others...including other professionals who are trying to build their business. If your attorney is not willing to recommend anyone, likely there is no one willing to recommend him/her.

☐ **When I call to ask questions, will you charge me?** Once you engage (hire) your attorney, you will be a billable client. You want to know when you will be billed and for how much.

☐ **What happens after I hire you?** If the Real Estate Attorney tells you nothing will need to happen until you get an offer, this is also a red flag. Your attorney should take the time to prepare and advise you on what to do and how to do it. He/she should have a conversation with you about your disclosures and what you want in your sales contract. This will ensure you are not making any mistakes up front that you will have to pay your attorney to fix. It will also ensure that you can turn the sales contract around quickly when you have an offer.

☐ **Where will the closing take place?** This is especially important if you have an attorney in another town. It is also important if you have a title company in the mix as the closing could take place at the title company's office.

☐ **(Optional) Can you also handle _____?** While attorneys have a specific scope of duties, they can also perform services outside of that scope for a fee. If you are uncomfortable in any aspect of the transaction, you can ask your attorney to handle that for you. For example, some sellers don't like to negotiate and they arrange for all offers to go through their attorney.

What To Do After Your Interviews

☐ **Make sure you receive the email follow up with the prices and services.** Bad follow up during the hiring process means bad follow up when you are closing.

☐ **Sign the letter of engagement.** This letter is your contract with the attorney and will outline services and prices. Do not be alarmed if your attorney does not use a letter of engagement.

☐ **Ask the attorney how disclosures work** in your state and find out what you are obligated to disclose.

☐ **Tell the attorney what is important to you for the sales contract and negotiation.** This could be price, a quick closing, not being present at the closing or numerous other items.

☐ **Ask how long it will take to turn around a sales contract once you get an offer.** This will let you set expectations for the buyer once you agree upon a price and terms for your house.

☐ **Ask the attorney for a form to fill out** once you get an offer to ensure the attorney has everything needed to write up the sales contract.

☐ **Add your attorney's phone number to your speed dial or phone contacts** so you can call the attorney immediately after you receive an offer...after you do your happy dance of course.

Bonus

Listen to my interview with a Real Estate Attorney explaining the process at www.fsboacademy.com/freebookbonus.

CHAPTER 3
HIRING A TITLE AGENT/COMPANY

Title companies can go by different names. Sometimes they are called Title Agents, Title Insurance Agents, or Closing Agents. Regardless, this company will research your title (deed to your property), provide title insurance to you as a seller, coordinate the closing, and handle the transfer of funds. From here on out, I'll refer to this company as the Title Agent.

Ideally, you will hire an attorney that can also act as the Title Agent. If you don't, that is okay. The process to hire a Title Agent is less involved than hiring a Real Estate Attorney. Why? Your attorney will advise you and guide you through the process. You will develop a relationship with the attorney. The Title Agent is performing a service for you, which is a more of a transactional relationship.

Finding the Title Agent

☐ Ask your Real Estate Attorney for a recommendation.
☐ Referrals from friends are second best. Post this message on the social media sites you use. "Does anyone know a good Title Company?"

Questions to Ask

Just like with a Real Estate Attorney, you want to hire a Title Agent with whom you can relate and communicate.

☐ **Can you explain the Real Estate process to me and the assistance you will provide at each stage?** You want an agent that can simplify things and explain them in terms you can understand. If you feel overwhelmed or confused after this question, this is a clear sign you should say, "Thank you for your time, good bye." The real estate sale process seems complicated but it is really easy. If someone makes it sound complicated, that is a red flag.

☐ **Can you go through the list of services you will provide me and the price for each service. Also make sure to tell me when I will be billed for each service?** When this question is answered, ask if the information could be emailed to you as well. This question will let you understand where your money is going and when you will have to make payments. Note that there are very few occasions where Title Agents are paid before the closing. Why? They control the money flow at the closing, so it is easy for them to pay themselves.

☐ **When I call to ask questions, will you charge me?** Once you engage (hire) your Title Agent, you want to know if there are going to be any surprise costs. There should not be, but you want to know ahead of time.

☐ **What happens after I hire you?** Unlike with a Real Estate Attorney, a Title Agent's work starts after you receive an offer. In some cases, the deposit may go to the Title Agent, other times it may go to the Real Estate Attorney. Ask both where the deposit goes. Both will charge you to escrow the money. If it can go to both, choose the cheaper of the two.

☐ **Where will the closing take place?** This will vary by state and locale. In some places, you close at the Title Agent's office and in others you close with an Attorney. I've also heard of people closing at the mortgage company or in their own house.

Once you are comfortable with a Title Agent, you can make your decision. In most cases there are no upfront contracts to sign until the work begins. Just make sure you know what to do once you receive an offer.

CHAPTER 4
PUTTING A PRICE TAG ON YOUR HOUSE

The number one decision that you will make is the selling price of your house. This will determine how much money you make from your house sale and how fast it sells.

Ways to Price Your House for Sale

Here are the different ways to price your house for sale - in order from worst to best.

1. **Guess** – You know your neighbor sold his house for $200,000, so you are going to sell your house for $200,000. Don't do this. Period, just don't do this.
2. **Determine the Profit You Want to Make** - You owe $150,000 on your house and you want to have $75,000 for a down payment, so you list your house for sale at $225,000. Don't do this. Your buyer does not care how much profit you need to make.
3. **Use an Online Estimator** – Many banking websites have free tools that let you enter your address and they will estimate the value of your house. There are also services that will charge you for this approach. Or, you go to Zillow® and use their Zestimator®. Don't do this. These estimators all use some really good data, but the data still needs human interpretation.
4. **Call a Real Estate Agent (or three)** – All Real Estate Agents are willing to come to your house and tell you how much they would list your house for sale. They do this free of charge with the hopes of landing you as a client. Be up front with them and tell them you are selling your house on your own. This won't dissuade them; it will just make them more determined. Ask more

than one agent, because each will have their own agenda. Do this to validate your research and only if you are comfortable. Quite frankly, I would not be comfortable doing this, but about half of the sellers I interviewed suggested this.

5. **Create Your Own Home Value Estimator System** – This is where you research how much houses have sold for in your area and for how much houses are currently selling. Document this information and analyze it. Do this. Doing this research on your own will give you a deep level of understanding about your local market. In fact, you will know more than most Real Estate Agents after conducting this research.

> **Bonus**
> You can get my step by step guide on how to do this and an Excel® template at www.fsboacademy.com/freebookbonus.

6. **GET AN APPRAISAL** – This is the best option when pricing your house for sale. Not only will you receive an unbiased opinion, you will receive an appraisal book that can be handed to buyers during the negotiation process to boost your position. An appraisal will cost about $350-$450. I did this when helping my Mom sell her house on her own. It cost $400, took about two weeks to coordinate, and provided us with a 50 page document detailing the property's value. It is a great negotiating tool.

How to Find An Appraiser

☐ Start by asking your Real Estate Attorney for Referrals.

☐ You can find certified appraisers at http://www.appraisers.org/find-an-appraiser
  o Note that some states also certify appraisers and those appraisers may not show up at Appraisers.org.

Questions To Ask An Appraiser

Depending on your location, an appraiser's job can be easy or tough. Regardless, you want to make sure you get an experienced appraiser.

☐ **How long have you been an appraiser?**

☐ **Are you certified? Through what organization?** Note that while the American Society of Appraisers certifies appraisers, so do some states. If an appraiser advises he/she is certified through the state, confirm if he/she is actually certified or only licensed through the state. Anyone can get licensed; however, certification usually requires experience, an exam and ongoing education.

o If not, how was the appraiser trained?

☐ **Can you walk me through how you would conduct the appraisal?**
Expect a longer answer from a good appraiser. If the response is short,
tell the appraiser you are new to this and ask for more details. One
appraiser I interviewed was very short with me, so I said thank you and
went to the next candidate.

☐ **How many houses have you appraised in the last year?**

☐ **What percentages of those have been in my area?** In smaller
towns, your appraiser may come from 30-50 miles away. While this is
not bad, there is a disadvantage of not living and working near you.

☐ **Can you send me a sample appraisal?** The appraiser may be taken
aback by this question, but ask for it anyway. If the appraiser is not
able to provide a sample appraisal, this alone is not enough to cross
them off your list.

☐ **How much do you charge? Is that a flat fee or do certain
variables increase the fee?** If you live in a community or in a city,
expect a flat fee. However if you have a lot of land, the price could
increase. Most appraisals are $350-$450.

**Question: Is it better to get an appraiser who is local and not
certified, or an appraiser who is from further away but is certified?**

I was faced with this exact question when hiring an appraiser for my
mother in Illinois. Illinois is a state where the appraisers are certified by the
state. I could hire a state certified appraiser who was local to the area or
hire an American Society of Appraisers (ASA) certified appraiser from
about 50 miles away. I ended up hiring the local appraiser because he had
been in business for 15 years. If he had not been in business for more than
a few years, I would have went with the ASA certified appraiser from
further away.

Getting The Highest Appraisal Amount

While the house appraisal is unbiased, you can influence it. An
appraiser will come to (and into) your house, conduct the inspection, and
take measurements. After he leaves your house, he will research your house
using several tools. He will view the price history of your house and the
history of other houses that have sold in your area. Here are some things
you can do to get the most favorable appraisal.

☐ **Make sure your house is clean and looks great.** First impressions
are important. It is human nature to think more highly of a house that
is clean and well-kept than one that is this dirty or has noticeable

damage.

☐ **Make all the repairs before the appraiser comes.** Let's face it; there are probably several things you have put off for years around your house that you will fix before selling it. It could be fixing that leaky faucet, repairing the missing fence board, or power washing the house. Do these before the appraiser comes. You don't want to get a poor review for a dirty house or repairs that are easy to complete.

☐ **Make his job easy.** Ensure the attic and crawlspaces are accessible. A good appraiser will look in every nook and cranny of your house. Keep the pets at bay and have the children go to a friend's house.

☐ **Create a list of every upgrade you have done since you bought the house.** Appraisers are going to rely heavily on past sales of your house. If you have completed any upgrades, make sure to have a list of them handy. While the appraiser is in the house, show him the upgrades. Once you are done showing him around the house, give him the list of upgrades. It is a nice bonus if you can include what you paid for each upgrade.

☐ **Provide him with past appraisals…if they are beneficial.** I lived in my last house for 10 years and had three appraisals completed. One when we purchased the house, one when we got a line of credit and one when we refinanced the house. When each appraiser came, I provided him a copy of the previous appraisal. Psychologically, this gave him an anchor for his pricing.

☐ **Provide the comps…and the non-comps.** You know your neighborhood and area better than any appraiser. If you are prudent, you have kept track of the sales prices of houses around you and know which ones are similar to yours and which are not. Provide the appraiser a list of comparable houses that have sold recently that are similar to yours. And if something should not be used, tell him as well. For example, "This house is just like mine, but their kids bought if from the parents at a great price." When the appraiser writes up his report, he will have to justify everything he puts in it.

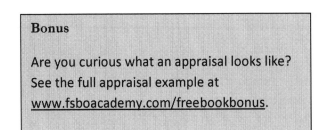

Bonus

Are you curious what an appraisal looks like?
See the full appraisal example at
www.fsboacademy.com/freebookbonus.

CHAPTER 5:
HOW TO PREPARE YOUR HOME FOR SALE

Next to pricing your house, the second most important action you can take to increase the value of your house is to make it look great. **Great looking houses will sell faster and for more money.** Houses that are not kept up will take much longer to sell and you will not get top dollar.

Even if you decide to sell your house through an agent (but I know you won't), you will still need to do these tasks. This will be the hardest part of selling your house. If you can hire professionals to come in and do the dirty work, I strongly recommend it.

The question I get asked the most about this stage, is "How do you know when you have your house ready to list. There is always one more thing you can do." You will know your house is ready when you say to yourself, "My house looks so good now, I'm not sure I want to sell it."

Preparing the Outside of Your House

☐ **Mow the grass.** You may need to mow a little more often than usual. Consider mowing on Fridays as much house hunting by working families takes place on the weekends.

☐ **Add sod if needed.** If you have dead areas of grass (like many of us do in the south), consider installing new sod. This is hard work, but it is an immediate fix. Just make sure you water it regularly.

☐ **Clean up the landscaping.** Trim your bushes and remove or replace any dead plants.

☐ **Pressure wash the house and walkways.** Alternatively you could use a hose and a brush and scrub the house. Better yet, hire a professional. You can hire someone to pressure wash your house at a cost of $100 and up – check local ads for service providers.

- ☐ **Don't forget the windows.** Clean them inside and out to let as much sunshine in as possible. Sunshine = Great Impression.
- ☐ **Pick up the dog poop!** It will save you from needing to clean up poop that was tracked in the house by the buyers and their agents.
- ☐ **Plant some seasonal flowers.** Plant them in beds around your mailbox, near the front door and in focal points of your front yard.
- ☐ **Clean up clutter.** Pick up any kids' toys and get rid of any old yard furniture. Make sure trash cans are put away, and garden hoses and equipment are neatly stored.
- ☐ **Clean up your entry way and make it sparse.** Buyers should be able to experience the full entry way when they step into it. Consider adding a fresh coat of paint to your front door, replacing rusted hardware and kick plates.

Preparing the Inside of Your House

- ☐ **Clean your walls.** Have your walls been painted in the last 5 years with high quality paint (not just what was on sale at Home Depot® or Lowes®)? Are the walls a neutral color? If you answered yes to both of these questions, you can simply wash your walls. All you need is bucket of warm soapy water and a hand towel. The best investment you will make during this process is to get a couple boxes of Magic Erasers.
- ☐ **Paint your walls.** If you answered no to either question above, then consider painting your walls before you sell your house on your own. Make sure to get neutral colors (light tan or gray). If you have rooms with bright colored walls or murals (yes, I've seen them), then you need to consider painting.
- ☐ **Clean and declutter the kitchen.** Make sure to wash down the cabinets and countertops. Shine up the plumbing fixtures. Clean inside and outside of major appliances (baby oil is great for shining and de-streaking stainless steel). Next, remove everything from the countertops. You can leave the coffee pot and maybe one or two other items at most.
- ☐ **Declutter the rest of the house.** Make sure you go through the rest of the house and declutter as well. Remove all personal items from the bathrooms and clean off the counters. If you have more than 2 items on a table or shelf, consider removing some. Clean out your closets and remove about 75% of the toys from your kids' rooms.
- ☐ **Don't forget the floors.** The two main focal points when someone is in your house will be the walls and floors. If you have carpet, clean it.

If it still looks bad after cleaning, consider replacing it with new carpet. If you replace the carpet, purchase a low to mid grade level and keep the colors neutral, but a little on the darker side. For example, choose a light tan over an off white. Replace cracked tiles and ripped vinyl flooring. If you have wood floors, consider getting them sanded and stained.

☐ **Finally, get rid of those odors.** If you smoke, start going outside to smoke. Try using some of the powdered carpet cleaners weekly to help keep odors out of the carpet. Don't leave smelly shoes in a laundry room or closet; put them in the garage. Cut down on cooking pungent foods. Alternatively, don't go overboard with artificial air fresheners, either.

CHAPTER 6
DISCLOSURES

In the course of selling your house, you need to disclose all material defects known by you. Disclosures can vary state by state, so be sure to hire a Real Estate Attorney to help guide you through this process.

Having a few things wrong with your house is not bad. Hiding them is bad. Disclosing them will build trust between you and the buyer. Compare selling your house to interviewing for a job. If you were asked what your weaknesses are, and you responded that you had none, the interviewer will not trust you. However, if you disclose your weaknesses you build trust with the interviewer.

Here are some areas to think about when writing up your disclosure:

Are the following in working condition?
- [ ] Refrigerator
- [ ] Microwave
- [ ] Range
- [ ] Oven
- [ ] Dishwasher
- [ ] Garbage Disposal
- [ ] Washer
- [ ] Dryer
- [ ] Ceiling fans
- [ ] Ceiling lights
- [ ] Garage door and opener
- [ ] Security system
- [ ] Water heater

- ☐ Water softener
- ☐ Pool & equipment
- ☐ Spa or hot tub
- ☐ Irrigation system
- ☐ Built in gas grill
- ☐ Sauna
- ☐ Fireplace
- ☐ Smoke detectors
- ☐ Windows
- ☐ Generators
- ☐ Fencing

Are you aware of any of the following?

- ☐ Legal actions affecting the property
- ☐ Tax liens on the property
- ☐ Any tax assessments affecting the property
- ☐ Have you been notified of any modifications to your property line
- ☐ Restrictions on the use of your property
- ☐ Pending legal action affecting the homeowners association
- ☐ Pending fee increases or assessments from the homeowners association
- ☐ Proposed changes to the homeowners covenants
- ☐ Resale restrictions
- ☐ Restrictions on renting or leasing
- ☐ Any natural mineral rights to the property and restrictions against them
- ☐ Current violations of the covenants
- ☐ Materials currently (or in the past) on the property such as asbestos
- ☐ Any recalls on the materials used to build the house
- ☐ Any wetlands on the property
- ☐ Buffers on the property
- ☐ Lead based paint used on the house or property
- ☐ Restrictions on access to public or private roads
- ☐ Structural damage to the property caused by fire, wind, flood, hail, sinkholes or other natural disaster
- ☐ Issues with property zoning
- ☐ Leaks in the roof
- ☐ Issues with the HVAC system (AC and Heat)
- ☐ Standing water on the property
- ☐ Current or past sinkholes on the property

- ☐ Foggy windows
- ☐ Problems with the plumbing system (leaky faucets, backups, etc.)
- ☐ Problems with the septic system
- ☐ Malfunctioning electrical switches or outlets
- ☐ Past or present termite/ant damage
- ☐ Restrictions on transferring bonds or warranties
- ☐ Flood zone restrictions

Provide a copy of the following:
- ☐ Homeowners Association covenants
- ☐ Fees for the homeowners association

Remolding & Alterations:
- ☐ Have there been any alterations to the property?
  - o Were all necessary permits obtained?
- ☐ Are there any active permits on the property?

Answer the following questions:
- ☐ Are your fees current?
- ☐ Are your taxes current?
- ☐ What is the age of the roof?
- ☐ What is the age of the AC unit?
- ☐ What is the age of the Heating system?
- ☐ Are there any items affixed to the property that are leased (i.e. Water Filtration System)?
- ☐ Does any person or organization have the right of first refusal to purchase the property?

Bonus

What to see an example of a disclosure document? You can see an example of a disclosure document at www.fsboacademy.com/freebookbonus. However, make sure you get your disclosure document from your attorney as they vary state by state.

CHAPTER 7:
TAKING AWESOME PICTURES

Your house will sell itself, but the pictures will bring the buyers to the door. You need to pay special attention to the pictures you post for your house.

Must Have Shots

Make sure to include these shots in your listing.

- ☐ Each room in the house
- ☐ Outside front of house
- ☐ Outside back of house
- ☐ Outside view into back yard
- ☐ Great front entrance shot
- ☐ Community common areas

Prepping Each Area

All Rooms
- ☐ Stage the house as much as possible
    - o Make sure the furniture fits the room (i.e. no desks in the bedroom)
    - o No more than 2 items on a table or shelf
    - o Clear off the bathroom counters and kitchen counters
    - o Straighten and arrange the furniture
- ☐ Clean windows inside and out
- ☐ Pick up clutter from the floors
- ☐ Vacuum, mop and dust

- ☐ Turn off ceiling fans
- ☐ Open the blinds and curtains
- ☐ Remove personal photos
- ☐ Nothing should be out of place
- ☐ Get the kids and pets out of the room
- ☐ Only have lights on if you need them (make sure all lights in a room have matching lightbulbs)

Kitchen
- ☐ Clear off the counters
- ☐ Clean off fridge (no magnets or papers)
- ☐ Empty the sink (no dishes, dish soap, sponges, etc.)
- ☐ Remove trash cans
- ☐ Remove pet bowls

Bathrooms
- ☐ Clear off the counters
- ☐ Open the shower curtain
- ☐ Remove all items from bath/shower
- ☐ Remove trash cans
- ☐ Remove plungers and toilet cleaners
- ☐ Close toilet seats

Bedrooms
- ☐ Clear off dressers
- ☐ Clear off side tables (max of 2 items on top of each)
- ☐ Turn off Televisions
- ☐ Remove exercise equipment
- ☐ Remove personal pictures
- ☐ Remove posters
- ☐ Put all clothes away
- ☐ Remove about 75% of your hanging clothes from the closet
- ☐ Remove shoes from the floor in the closet
- ☐ Make the bed

Laundry Room
- ☐ Put away all laundry
- ☐ Close the washer and dryer
- ☐ Hide the detergent

☐ Clear off washer and dryer

Common Areas
☐ Clear off side tables (max of 2 items on top of each)
☐ Clear off desks
☐ Turn off Televisions
☐ Remove exercise equipment
☐ Put coats away
☐ Remove personal pictures

Outside
☐ Mow the grass
☐ Trim the bushes
☐ Remove all toys
☐ Remove any worn out lawn furniture
☐ Sweep sidewalks and driveways
☐ Move cars
☐ Remove the for sale sign
☐ Clean the pool
☐ Remove any tools
☐ Hide trash and recycling bins

Bonus

Check out examples of some great photos that were taken after the house was staged by the seller. These pictures helped sell the house in just three days - www.fsboacademy.com/freebookbonus.

Tips for Great Shots

☐ Pictures should be taken on a bright sunny day.
☐ Use a website like http://apps.pixlr.com/editor/ to adjust the photo's brightness.
☐ Take photos from eye level.
☐ Use a tripod.

- ☐ A good camera phone is okay to use – make sure the pictures are taken with the phone held sideways, not up and down. You want your pictures to be wide, not tall.
- ☐ Take pictures with both lights off and lights on.
- ☐ Set the table with the good china…just like Martha Stewart would do.
- ☐ Shoot rooms from many different angles/corners (at least 4 angles).
- ☐ Outside shots look better from angles than straight on.
- ☐ Make sure your shots are level and your lines in the room run straight.
- ☐ Use a camera with a wide angle lens or purchase a phone accessory for small rooms if you have one (or try just a panorama setting).

CHAPTER 8
CREATING YOUR LISTING

In 2014, 92% of buyers used the internet to search for houses according to the National Association of Realtors. You must be online if you are going to sell your house today.

Where To List Your House
1. www.zillow.com – Zillow is the number one real estate site in the world – even more popular than Realtor.com. When it comes to online listing, Zillow is the only place you need to be.
2. Realtor.com – Once you list your house on the MLS system, it will be added to Realtor.com automatically. Don't waste your money paying for a listing here.

Pictures to Include

Most buyers will spend the bulk of their time looking at the pictures you post. Include as many pictures as possible, but at minimum, include one of every room. As a bonus, include multiple pictures for each room from different angles.

☐ Front of House
☐ Back of House
☐ View from back porch
☐ Kitchen
☐ Each Bathroom
☐ Each Bedroom
☐ Living Room
☐ Basement

- ☐ Breakfast nook
- ☐ All other rooms
- ☐ Pool
- ☐ Community amenities
- ☐ A layout of your house (showing where the rooms are and their sizes)
- ☐ A layout of your lot showing the house structure and the lot boundaries
- ☐ Any exquisite features of your house

Bonus

To see what a floorplan and a lot plan look like, check out our free bonus resources at www.fsboacademy.com/freebookbonus.

What To Include In The Write Up

Your write up is secondary to your pictures so don't get hung up here. Keep it simple seller (KISS).

Start with a short description of the house - *This 3 bedroom, 2 bathroom, 1,400 square foot ranch style house is located in small subdivision.*

Highlight the exquisite features of the house - *The house sits on top of a finished basement, has an in-ground pool, and a 3 car garage.*

Talk about what you will miss when you move - *The current owners will miss the quietness of the neighborhood and all the friendly neighbors.*

Identify for whom the house would be perfect - *This house is perfect for a new family who wants to send their kids to great schools or grandparents that want to spend a lot of time with their grandkids.*

If you get stuck on this portion, start by filling in the blanks below. Then post it to Facebook to get feedback from your friends.

This __ bedroom, __ bathroom (Style of House) is located (what is special about the location). The house has (list 2-3 special features about the house, like a chef's kitchen or a new roof). The owners will miss (1-2 things you will miss when you move). This house is perfect for someone who _____.

Post this listing on Facebook once you are finished starting with the comment, "*I need some help from my friends who have been to my house before. Below is the first draft of the listing for my house. Putting yourself in my shoes, how would you rewrite this?*" Then copy and paste what you write in the above template.

Wait...You Are Not Done Yet

When conducting my interviews with people selling their own houses, I always email them from their house listing to give them heads up that I am going to call. About half the time, they tell me they never received my email. Yikes! How many of their potential buyers are going into junk mail? Follow these steps to keep this from happening to you.

- ☐ Find your listing on Zillow.com, make sure your phone number is correct and email yourself for more information.
- ☐ Look in your email for the notification. When you find it (may be in spam or junk folder), add the address to your address book.
- ☐ Repeat the steps above for the other sites (Fizber, Craigslist, etc.).

CHAPTER 9:
SIGNS AND FLYERS

You are going to get online traffic and offline traffic coming to your house. Post your house on the internet to get the online traffic and post signs and flyers to generate offline traffic.

Signs

Signs will help buyers find your house. You want to place one sign in front of your house and place signs at all major intersections with arrows pointing the way to your house. Always ask for permission before placing a sign on private property and follow your HOA rules when it comes to real estate signs. The same advice goes for open house signs.

The Front Yard Sign

You can go to your local hardware store and purchase a sign, buy one from Amazon (Affiliate Link: http://amzn.to/1f638pZ) or order a custom sign from Signs.com. All are good choices. Remember, it is not your sign that is going to sell the house; it is the house itself and the price.

- [ ] **Include your phone number** in large legible print on the sign.
- [ ] **Do not write the price on the sign.** Only include the price on the flyer, as it may change later.
- [ ] **Make your sign easily accessible** by placing the sign within one step from the sidewalk or side of the road.
- [ ] If you live on a corner lot, **consider one sign for each road.**
- [ ] **Include a holder for your flyers.**
- [ ] **Include Sign Riders.** Sign riders are mini signs that you add on to

your sign to point out important features such as those below.
- o Pool
- o Warranty
- o Open House

Directional Signs

While most of your traffic will come from the internet, some will come from people driving around. In these cases, you want to direct their car in your direction. Make sure you put up enough directional signs and follow these tips.

- ☐ **Use signs to reassure the driver that they are still going in the right direction.** Signs should be no more than 1/8 of a mile apart from each other.
- ☐ **Place signs at all major roads and intersections** that are nearest to your house.
- ☐ **Place a sign at every required turn.**
- ☐ **Skip writing the address on the sign as drivers will not be able to read it anyway.** Consider writing the subdivision name or part of town instead.
- ☐ **Make sure your directional signs and yard sign are similar.** If you have a red yard sign, don't get blue directional signs. If your yard sign is rectangular, don't get house shaped directional signs.

Flyers

The purpose of a flyer is twofold. First, place it in-front of your house so passersbys (and nosey neighbors) can learn more about your house. Second, place the flyer in public spaces to drive traffic to your house…literally.

Here are some tips to help you.

- ☐ **Use www.canva.com to create your real estate flyers.** This is a free site that makes this super easy.
- ☐ **Have more pictures than words.** When you look at your flyer, make sure the majority of the flyer is covered in pictures of your house, not words.
- ☐ **At minimum, include the front view of your house and your other two best photos.** It does not matter what room they are, just make sure they can wow the buyer.

☐ **Include the following details about your house**...in order of importance (You don't have to include everything).
1. Your First Name and Phone Number
2. Address
3. Link to online listing
   o Link to your Zillow page and use a URL shortener, like www.tinyurl.com, to make it easy for the buyer to type the address in their phone. I like TinyURL because you can use a custom extension. Use your street address so your URL looks like www.tinyurl.com/123mainstreet.
4. Price (and appraised value if you have it)
5. Number of bedrooms and bathrooms
6. Square footage
7. Note anything else that is special about the house, such as a pool, land, finished basement, bonus rooms, etc.

☐ **Print the flyers in color.** Remember, you want to wow the buyer here. You can check out http://www.nextdayflyers.com/flyer-printing/full-page-flyers.php to get an estimate on your printing and shipping costs. You should be able to get 100 copies for about $110. This is using glossy paper, full color on the front side and black and white on the back side.

☐ **Buy a holder in which to place your flyers.** Check out this one on Amazon (Affiliate Link: http://amzn.to/1B9OyHC) and attach it to your sign using zip ties.

☐ **See the Finding the Right Buyers Chapter for ideas on where to distribute flyers.**

☐ ALWAYS tell the buyer how to make an offer. Feel free to use this verbiage on the back of the flyer.

Do you want to make an offer or schedule a showing?

Do you have an agent? Great - give your agent this flyer and your agent can call me to set up a showing or make an offer. Don't worry; we will pay your agent's commission.

Don't have an agent? Great - we both will save some additional money. Once you are ready for a showing or to make an offer, just give me a call. If you are setting up a showing, we will find a time that is convenient for you — note you must be pre-approved for a mortgage at list price before the showing. If you are ready to make an offer, please have a dollar amount in mind for the offer and let me *know any stipulations. Once we reach an agreement (this may take a few phone calls), I will forward the details to my Real Estate Attorney. My attorney will write up a sales contract for you to sign. You will send the contract and the deposit ($1,000) to the attorney and I will countersign the contract. Once we both sign the contract, you will provide a copy of the contract to your mortgage company and they will lead you through the rest of the process. You will always be able to call me and ask questions throughout the process as well. I look forward to hearing from you in the next day or two.*

Bonus

You can get a PDF copy of this verbiage to upload along with the front side of your flyer at www.fsboacademy.com/freebookbonus.

Here is a great example of a flyer over at Canva.com

CHAPTER 10
FINDING THE RIGHT BUYERS

You don't want to find buyers; you want to find THE right buyer. Ninety percent (90%) of your marketing is going to come from listing your house online via Zillow or the MLS system (more about the MLS in a minute). However, there are some things you can do in order increase the number of people who are aware that your house is for sale.

Using Social Media

Social Media can be a timewaster but you can turn it into a money maker when selling your house. Try these tips.

- [ ] **Stick to the social websites you already use.**
- [ ] **Post pictures.**
- [ ] **Space out your postings.** Post something about your house every 4-5 days.
- [ ] **Ask your friends to share your posts.**
- [ ] **Start Early.** As you are taking your pictures, take several of each room. Post the best 3-4 pictures of a room and ask your friends to comment on which one you should use. Do the same with your listing write-up. The more your friends comment on your posts, the more likely they are to see future posts of yours.
- [ ] **Be grateful.** Thank everyone who helps you and be specific. People appreciate gratitude and it will encourage them to help you more.
- [ ] **Look for local community pages** that allow you to post details about your house (don't forget your church page if they allow it).
- [ ] **Link back to your Zillow listing.**
- [ ] **Create a story around your house.** Post a picture, tell a story about

the house and remind people it is for sale.

☐ **Post about events that are happening in your neighborhood** or town and remind people your house is for sale.

Using Your Friends & Neighbors

Engaging your friends and neighbors online is good, but engaging them offline is better.

☐ **Offer a cash incentive.** When talking to your friends and neighbors, tell them that you will pay them if they refer the person that buys your house. Give them a specific dollar amount. I'd recommend that you offer 0.5%. If you are selling your house for $100,000 then offer $500. If you are selling your house for $250,000 then offer $1,200 to $1,500. Also consider giving a small gift or gift card to anyone who gives you a referral.

☐ **Offer a different reward than money.** Some people may be uncomfortable taking money from you, so be creative. You could offer tickets for a sporting or theater event, a weekend stay at a bed and breakfast, a round of golf at a high end country club, or even to pay their mortgage for a month.

☐ **Take flyers around to your neighbors.** There is a good chance that your neighbors have had someone over to their house who commented, "I love this area." Knock on as many doors as possible in your neighborhood and ask them if they know anyone who may be looking to move into the neighborhood. Offer them a flyer (or two or three) and tell them about your incentive.

☐ **Host a Multi Family Yard Sale.** Having a yard sale will get a lot of people to come by your house. Hosting a multi-family yard sale will get a lot more people to come by your house. The more stuff you have, the more people will come. The more families you have contributing, the more people they will tell. Be prepared to have plenty of help as you may be giving tours of your house all morning.

☐ **Tell your coworkers** that you are moving and keep flyers at your desk (or posted in your work area, if allowed).

☐ **Tell people at your church or synagogue** you are moving and take flyers to services with you. Also see if there is a community bulletin board where you can post a flyer.

☐ **Tell other parents** your house is for sale when attending kids' events.

☐ **Host parties at your house.** These could be birthday parties, pool parties, 4th of July or Labor Day cookouts, or cookie exchanges. There is a reason to get together for every season.

Ideas on Where to Place Flyers

You want to place flyers around town in as many places as possible. Here are a few ideas to get you thinking of places to go. Always ask business owners before putting up flyers and don't forget to check back every week to see if you need to replace your flyer.

- ☐ Breakroom at your office
- ☐ Local grocery stores
- ☐ Your dry cleaner
- ☐ Local coffee shop
- ☐ Golf and Country clubs
- ☐ Neighborhood club house
- ☐ Church
- ☐ Child's school
- ☐ Nursing homes
- ☐ Places where you dine out
- ☐ Your gym
- ☐ Auto mechanics & oil changing businesses (really any place someone has to wait)
- ☐ Drop off to HR departments for large local businesses
- ☐ Local Real Estate offices (make sure to note you will pay buyer's commission)

Open Houses

To be honest with you, I am on the fence on whether open houses help sell a house. I have Real Estate Agent friends who have told me that they hold open houses as a means to find new buyer clients, not to sell your house. Alternatively, I have interviewed many sellers who found their buyer through an open house. If you have the time and are not getting enough traffic, try an open house. But don't fret if you decide not to have an open house.

Advertising the Open House

- ☐ **Update Zillow** with the time and date of the open house a couple of nights before (usually Wednesday or Thursday night). Zillow will send an email to anyone looking for houses in your area and notify them of the open house.

- ☐ **Advertise on Craigslist.** Normally, I would not advertise anything on Craigslist except the free stuff I want to put on the curb. However, many of the investors I've interviewed put an ad on Craigslist to advertise their open house.
- ☐ **Post notices to your social media sites** and ask your friends to share them. Also post it on community groups as well.
- ☐ **Create a new flyer** with the date and time of the open house and redistribute it.

Preparing for the Open House

- ☐ Deep clean the house.
- ☐ Open the curtains and blinds to let as much natural light in the house as possible.
- ☐ Turn on all the lights.
- ☐ Make sure the temperature is set to a comfortable level – 72 in the summer and 78 in the winter.
- ☐ Clear off the kitchen counters.
- ☐ Take out the trash.
- ☐ Clear off the bathroom counters.
- ☐ Put all laundry away.
- ☐ Open the pool and clean it out.
- ☐ Straighten up all bedrooms.
- ☐ Put all dishes in the dishwasher and run it.
- ☐ Lock up your valuables, don't just hide them. Consider getting a safe-deposit box.
- ☐ Don't cook breakfast that morning – you don't want the smells to linger.
- ☐ Leave out copies of any supporting documents, such as the appraisal, inspection, warranty, or brochures.
- ☐ Spray air freshener or light candles a half hour before the start of the event. Try to use something light and seasonal.
- ☐ Get the pets out of the house.
- ☐ Get the kids out of the house.

Conducting Your Open House

- ☐ Safety First – Never conduct an open house alone.
- ☐ Smile a lot and be kind.
- ☐ Plan on people showing up early…usually a half hour. These buyers

may be extra interested in buying your house.

- [ ] Ask a local mortgage professional to print up a rate sheet for your house. Give it to buyers who are not preapproved.
- [ ] Greet each person at the front door.
- [ ] Ask questions to learn about your prospective buyers.
  - o What made you stop by today?
  - o How far along in the process are you?
  - o Have you been preapproved for a mortgage yet?
  - o Are you using an agent?
  - o What are you looking for in a house?
- [ ] Only one person should show them the house. The other partner should stay in the kitchen or living room.
- [ ] Allow the buyers to enter each room first. This allows them an unobstructed view of the area.
- [ ] If the couple you are showing the house to splits up, then your partner should engage and "help" the other person.
- [ ] If two couples show up at a time, split up and each of you take a couple around.
- [ ] If three or more couples show up at the same time, ask all the couples to wait in one area. One of you should engage them in small talk and the other can give tours one at a time.
  - o Small talk topics include: How did you find out about the open house? Do you have kids? Do you live around here? Where are you from? What do you do for a living?
- [ ] Once each tour is finished, make sure they leave with a flyer and questionnaire.
- [ ] Give the couple a short questionnaire and pen. Ask them to fill it out outside and place it in your mailbox.
  1. What was your overall impression of the house?
  2. What did you like about the house?
  3. What didn't you like about the house?
  4. What did you think of the price?

Host an Open House for Real Estate Agents

Since Real Estate Agents are allowed to pester you, you can pester them. You may want to host an open house just for Real Estate Agents. Here are some tips.

- [ ] **Host it during the week during business hours.** You want to target full time Real Estate Agents.

- **Stop by and drop off special flyers** to the local Real Estate Offices in town
- **Offer snacks and drinks** (mimosas in the morning and beer and wine in the afternoon, along with non-alcoholic beverages like coffee and tea)
- **Provide value to the agents.** The agents are likely going to begrudge you for not using an agent in the first place, so figure out a way to add value to their business. If you have a friend who is good at online marketing, ask him/her to host a short seminar at your house. This is a hot topic among Real Estate Agents right now. Other ideas could include short seminars from accountants, your real estate attorney, your appraiser, or a life coach. Also think about topics on diet, exercise, parenting, or meditation. Be creative!
- **Give the agents a tour** of your house and let them roam free.

The MLS System

The one advantage that Real Estate Agents have is the MLS (Multiple Listing Service). This is an agent controlled network that lists houses for sale. Listing your house on the MLS exposes your house to a wider audience. While many buyers can find your house online via Zillow, most agents won't bother with your house unless it is in the MLS database. The MLS also tells the buyer's agent that you are willing to pay their commission. I recommend paying the buyer's agent 2-3%.

- If you need to sell fast, list your house on the MLS out of the gate.
- If you don't need to sell your house right away, forego the MLS listing at first. You can always add it later.
- A MLS listing will cost you $200 - $400. There are online services such as www.fizber.com that offer this service.
- Contact a local agent and ask if he/she is willing to list your house on the MLS for $100. Most will want a little more than that, but start low in your offer to get a great deal.
- Consider listing on the MLS if traffic dies down on your house. It is a lot cheaper to spend $400 on an MLS listing than to lower the price of your house by a few thousand dollars.
- The MLS is local. When the national companies, such as Fizber and ForSaleByOwner.com offer these services, they are simply taking your money and outsourcing your listing to a local broker.

How Much Traffic Should I Expect?

☐ Calls and showings will be most frequent when you first list your house for sale.

☐ Houses sell the fastest during the summer. Expect things to slow down in the fall, go really slow in the winter, and start to pick up again in the spring.

☐ Anticipate 1-2 calls a week. Hopefully you will get a lot more, but you may get less.

☐ You will have some dry spells. You may go for three weeks without any calls. Be patient.

What To Do When You Are Stuck

☐ List your house on the MLS before lowering your price.

☐ If you get a lot of calls, but no showings, you need to lower your price (or make your home sound more appealing on the phone).

☐ If you go more than three weeks without getting any calls, consider the MLS or lowering your price.

☐ If you have 10-12 showings and don't get any offers, you either need to improve the look of your house or lower your price.

☐ If calls start to dry up, revisit the section on Finding The Right Buyers and try some new tactics.

☐ Visit open houses and find out what the other houses have that yours doesn't have.

☐ Don't be afraid to call a Real Estate Agent to get their opinion. The agent may give you some good ideas on how to improve things. Yes, they are going to try to get your business so stay strong. You have already done all the work. If you are already on the MLS, the only thing a Real Estate Agent can do to sell your house faster is to keep pestering you to lower your price. You'll pay a hefty 3% for this pestering.

☐ Hire a House Stager to come to your house and provide ideas on how to make your home look more attractive to buyers.

☐ Be Patient. You will have dry spells and this is normal.

Going Above and Beyond

Here are a few ideas to help you wow buyers or ease their fear of the buying process.

☐ **House Warranties** – Depending on the age of your house, you can get a house warranty for under $1,000. If you have a house that is more than a couple of years old, consider buying a warranty to remove the "risk" for the buyer.

☐ **Appraisals** – Having a certified third party evaluate your house can give great comfort to a buyer by letting the buyer know that he/she is not overpaying. Appraisals usually cost around $400.

☐ **Professional Photography** – Taking good pictures of your house is easy. Taking great pictures, where the lighting and angles are just right, can be difficult. For about $400, a professional photographer will take the pictures of your house.

☐ **House Inspections** – Paying for your own house inspection helps put buyers at ease, knowing that any flaws are out in the open.

☐ **Closing Costs Assistance** – Buying a house is expensive, and many buyers become strapped for cash. Offering to pay all or some of the closing costs can attract a wider variety of buyers.

☐ **Concessions for New (fill in the blank)** – Concessions are offering the buyer cash back at closing to pay for upgrading or fixing something. Oftentimes sellers will offer the buyer some cash back at closing to pay for something that needs repair or replacement. This is typically a poor idea. Most buyers want a move in ready house. Needing to purchase and oversee the installation of carpet will put off some buyers. I advise you to use concessions sparingly.

CHAPTER 11:
TYPES OF CALLS YOU WILL RECEIVE: HOW TO IDENTIFY & DEAL WITH EACH

As soon as you list your house for sale, you will get a flood of phone calls...many from the wrong people. From the people I've interviewed, the level and mix of calls is all over the place. Some reported a couple of calls from the "undesirables" to over 40 calls throughout the whole process. Don't fret about this though. As long as you know how to handle each call, this will only be a minor annoyance.

Here are the types of callers you will hear from:
- Real estate agents who want your business
- Investors who want a deal
- Renters
- Tire kickers
- Interested buyers without a real estate agent
- Interested buyers with a real estate agent

IMPORTANT NOTE: The more information you put online about your house, the fewer phone calls you will get. This is a good thing. You only want calls from interested buyers who can afford and want to buy your house. If you do a great job of putting information online, you will eliminate calls and showings from individuals who are not going to make you an offer.

Questions to Identify Your Caller

How may I help you?

The answer to this question will usually let you know the type of caller. Listen closely. If you still don't know, continue with these questions:

Do you intend to get a Real Estate Agent?

Agents should identify themselves at this point.

Renters and tire kickers will not have a Real Estate Agent and will try to dance around this question.

Investors typically use an agent to buy a house, but then sell it on their own. However, they will do most the leg work themselves. They include the agent in the buy so the agent can get the commission as payback for helping them find properties to invest in.

Some legitimate buyers want to buy the house without an agent to save money. They will let you know this.

Do you have a preapproval letter from a mortgage company? If paying in cash, do you have a bank statement you can send me to confirm you have the funds?

Tell the buyer that you would be happy to show the house once they have the preapproval letter or cash in the bank. Renters and tire kickers will not have this letter. If someone says he is selling his house and will use the proceeds from his house to pay for yours in cash, go with your gut here. You have the right to ask for a copy of their mortgage payoff letter to ensure their asking price will pay off the house and provide them with ample funds to purchase your house.

Are you looking to buy a house that you will move into, or are you going to rent or resell the house?

If there are any doubts left, this will flush out your investors.

Real Estate Agents Who Want Your Business

☐ Tell the agent you have a friend/family member who is a Real Estate Agent and if you decide to list with an agent, you've promised to use that person. This will discourage them from pursuing your business.

42

☐ If you don't want to hear from the agent again, ask for his/her name and then ask to be put on their Do Not Call List. Once you do this, they can be fined for calling you again.

☐ Many agents will want to "come see your house so they can tell other agents about it." Warning! This is a ploy to continue pitching their services to you. Insist that they bring an approved buyer, proven by a preapproval letter. An agent has no incentive to tell another agent about your house because they will not get commission for doing so.

☐ Having a few agents come by your house and conducting a market analysis for you is a good thing. Of course, they are going to try to get your listing. However, you can get a qualified opinion on your house and price by doing this. Just make sure the agent is a full time agent.

Investors Who Want A Deal

It is hard to go anywhere these days without seeing a sign telling you that someone will buy your house. My wife will buy your house or my dog will buy your house. (Just kidding about the dog, but you get the picture.) That is because there are a lot of investors out there looking for a good deal. While these investors are buyers, they are usually a waste of time if you know what you are doing. For a fun read, check out my article at http://www.fsboacademy.com/earn-extra-money-list-house-ways-handle-real-estate-investor-solicitations/

☐ Once you learn the person on the phone is an investor, tell them that you are not willing to entertain any offers that are below 90% of your asking price. A typical investor is usually looking to get a house for 70% or less than the amount they can get for reselling it.

☐ If they agree to that, consider showing them your house. Investors are usually one of the first people to call so this gives you a chance to practice showing your house. Also, listen carefully to what they have to say. The investor's feedback will be nitpicky because they want to drive the price down, so take it with a grain of salt. But listen closely. He/she may point out some things about your house of which you were not aware.

Renters

This is a new one for me and it just started popping up in my last round of interviews. Maybe that's because in some places rentals are in demand, or it could have just been the time of year. Regardless, think long and hard about whether you want to rent your house or sell it. The vast majority of you are going to want to sell your house. If you decide that renting is desirable, your Real Estate Attorney can help you with the paperwork.

☐ The best way to deter renters from calling you is to add this line to your listing write-up.
> *Will not consider offers for rent or rent to own. All buyers must be pre-approved for a mortgage or have a bank statement showing the money is in the bank.*

Tire Kickers

Tire kickers can be some of the toughest to identify and the biggest waste of your time. Most sellers won't want to "turn away" any potential buyers. Let's face it, if you are getting lots of activity, phone calls and showings, you feel good about your house. Try to fight this urge. You are going to be happier in the end if you stick to your guns and weed out the undesirables.

☐ Make sure to ask all the questions above.
☐ Under NO circumstances, allow someone to see your house without a preapproval letter or a copy of their bank statement confirming the funds are available. Make sure to get this ahead of time or cancel the showing.

Interested Buyers - Someone Who Really Wants To Buy Your House

The cream of the crop is an interested, approved buyer, without a Real Estate Agent.

☐ **Return all calls within an hour** – When buyers call you they are excited. You don't want to lose this excitement. Return calls promptly to ensure they see your house before they settle for another.
☐ **Be flexible** – Selling a house is stressful…and so is buying one. This is a big decision for your buyers, so you want to be as flexible as possible as long as you keep the deal moving forward. Be willing to do things like allowing the buyer to come over at the last minute and see the house again, answer questions that you feel you've already answered, or consider their requests during the negotiation. Remember, these buyers are looking at 10 or more houses and it can sometimes get confusing. Ask yourself, "Will this get me closer to making a deal?" If the answer is "Yes", then try to do what is requested.
☐ **Be organized** – When was the last time you went into a store that was

a mess? Did you buy anything? You probably bought nothing or a lot less than you would have in a nice, neat store. This advice extends to the look of your house AND to how you approach the deal. Have the questionnaire from the real estate attorney ready and make sure you get all the answers in one conversation. Have a packet of information ready for the buyer that includes all the pertinent documents.

Real Estate Agents Who Represent a Particular Interested Buyer

Most buyers use a Real Estate Agent when purchasing a house. Why? They don't have to pay the buyer's commission. They get free advice on your dime. That is okay, because you are still saving the 3% commission that you would have paid an agent to represent you.

- ☐ **Remember that the agent is just a go-between.** Outside of advising you, there is not much heavy lifting that an agent does besides relaying the buyer's wants and desires to the seller. Keep this in mind. It is likely that any question or request made by the agent came from the buyer.

- ☐ **Ask Questions.** Don't be afraid to ask any type of question to the buyer's agent.
  - o You can ask them things about the buyer (i.e. Why are they moving? Do they have kids? What don't the like about the house?).
  - o You can ask them about the process. Your best advisor is your Real Estate Attorney, but you can ask the buyer's agent questions, too. For example, what is the difference between a VA loan and a regular loan?
  - o You can ask them to do tasks for you. For example, if the buyer calls you and wants to come by to take measurements, ask their agent to meet the buyer at the house if you cannot be around.

- ☐ **Not all agents are good.** I've heard many horror stories about disorganized and lazy agents. One attorney I interviewed told me how an agent never delivered the disclosures to the buyer. The buyer later discovered something that was wrong with the house and sued the seller. Long story short, micromanage the buyer's agent to make sure everything is done correctly.

CHAPTER 12
SHOWING YOUR HOUSE

Showing your house is where the sale is made. Your house is going to sell itself, but there are some things you can do to help this process along for both you and your buyer. In general, here is how the process will work:

1. Buyer or agent calls you to ask questions about the house.
2. Answer their questions and then ask some important questions of your own.
3. Schedule a date and time to show your house.
4. Clean and prepare your house before the showing.
5. Show your house.
    a. If the buyer has an agent, you will leave the house and the buyer's agent will show the house.
    b. If the buyer does not have an agent, you will show the house to the buyer.
6. Get feedback from the buyer.

Once you start showing your house, it is a numbers game. Expect to show your house about 8-10 times before you get an offer to sell. This will differ greatly by house and area of course. I estimate 8-10 as the number of times though, because in 2014, the average buyer looked at 10 houses. If you show your house 10-12 times and do not get an offer, it is time to take a look at your price and house to determine what needs to change. Don't be surprised if you get low ball offers and don't be surprised if you get people asking if you are willing to rent your house.

Talking to the Buyer or Their Agent

There is not much difference between talking to a buyer directly or to a buyer's agent. With a buyer's agent, you can be direct in asking your questions. With the buyer though, you want to be more conversational.

- ☐ Answer all their questions and be patient.
- ☐ Be polite, no matter what mood you are in.
- ☐ Return all calls immediately. You do not want to let excitement fade.
- ☐ Make sure you minimize background noise (television, clanking of dishes, barking dogs, etc.).
- ☐ Ask Questions:
  - o Will the buyer be taking out a mortgage or paying cash? You want to make sure you are only showing your house to people who can afford to buy your house.
    - If Mortgage – Do you have a preapproval letter in hand? If not, this will be required before the showing.
    - If Cash – Do you have a copy of the bank statement in hand showing the funds are in the account? If not, this will be required before the showing.
    - If Selling A House Then Paying Cash – Can you provide a copy of your current mortgage statement so I can verify that you will have enough left over to buy my house?
  - o If the buyers are not preapproved, they are not serious buyers. Tell the buyer/agent that you recommend that they keep an eye out for any future open houses and they can stop by then.
  - o What is their timeline for closing? Do they have another house that needs to be sold before closing?
  - o What are their "must haves" in their new house?
  - o Will you be able to provide feedback within 24 hours of the showing from the buyers?
    - Feedback is very important for you to understand the market's opinion of your house.
- ☐ Repeat the date and time back to the buyer/agent. Ask for a cell phone number you can call in case something comes up and provide yours as well.
- ☐ Call to confirm 24 hours in advance of the appointment. Most of your appointments will be the following day and don't be surprised if the buyer asks to stop by now or in a couple of hours.
- ☐ If you get a last minute request to show your house and you cannot get home to clean and tidy up, go ahead and show it anyway. Most buyers

who ask for last minute showings will understand any clutter. However, the best thing to do is tidy up a little before you leave the house each morning so you'll be prepared for surprise showings.

☐ Provide the buyer's agent with the code to the lock box (more about that later).

☐ As soon as you hang up the phone, Google the agent to make sure that they are legitimate. If you have any questions about their legitimacy, change the key code and cancel the showing.

The Day of the Showing

Let's face it, showing your house can be a pain in the butt. You have to clean, make arrangements for your pets and kids, and sometimes find something to do for two hours. Here are some tips to make your showing as successful as possible.

☐ Open the curtains and blinds to let as much natural light in the house as possible.

☐ Turn on all the lights.

☐ Make sure the temperature is set to a comfortable level – 72 in the summer and 78 in the winter.

☐ Clear off the kitchen counters.

☐ Take out the trash.

☐ Clear off the bathroom counters.

☐ Put all laundry away.

☐ Open the pool and clean it out.

☐ Straighten up all bedrooms.

☐ Put all dishes in the dishwasher and run it.

☐ Lock up your valuables, don't just hide them. Consider getting a safe-deposit box.

☐ Don't cook breakfast that morning – you don't want the smells to linger.

☐ Leave copies of any supporting documents you created, such as the appraisal, inspection, warranty, or brochures.

☐ Spray a light air freshener about a half hour before the showing or before you leave the house.

☐ Get the pets out of the house.

☐ If the buyer has an agent, leave the house a half hour before the showing and return an hour after the scheduled start time.

Showing Your House with a Buyer's Agent

If the buyer has an agent, the buyer's agent will show your house, not you. Make sure to spend a little extra time on the phone with the agent telling the agent about what makes your house so great. For access to your house, you can either leave the door unlocked (a fine approach if you are normally home during the day) or provide the agent with the code to your lock box.

Note that I do not recommend giving out your garage code to an agent for safety reasons. Besides, your house looks best entering from the front door, not your garage.

A few hours after the showing is complete, call the agent and ask for feedback.

- ☐ What was the buyer's overall impression of the house?
- ☐ What did they like about the house?
- ☐ What didn't they like about the house?
- ☐ What did they think of the price?
- ☐ Do you think they will make an offer?

Showing Your House To The Buyer Directly

Showing your own house can be lots of fun and you can get some great feedback. Follow this advice as you conduct your showing and you can't miss.

- ☐ Never show the house by yourself, especially if you are a woman. While the chances of a crime occurring are very low when you are showing your house, think safety first. If your spouse or partner is not available, ask a neighbor or friend to stop by and help. If you have neighborhood security, you could request they drive by a few times during the showing as well.
- ☐ Meet the buyers outside and engage in small talk. Find out what they are looking for, why they are moving, and where they are in their process. This will help you customize your presentation on the tour.
- ☐ Showcase the best parts of your house last. You want the buyers to leave with a great impression.
- ☐ Be honest. Your house will sell itself and buyers don't expect the house to be perfect. Highlighting something that is wrong with the house will help build trust between you and the buyer.

- ☐ Keep the buyers in sight at all times. You don't have to be right on top of them, just within eyesight.
- ☐ Don't forget to show them the neighborhood's amenities, such as the pool, clubhouse and tennis courts. This may be a good place to start as it is in a public place.
- ☐ Pick 1-2 items in each room to highlight.
- ☐ Plant ideas of what each room could be based on your knowledge of the buyer. For example, if they are expecting a baby, show them what room could be the nursery. If one of them works from home, show them which room could be a good office.
- ☐ Provide a takeaway packet for the house.
  - o Copy of the house flyer at minimum with your phone number and directions on how to make an offer. Feel free to use this verbiage. *Thank you so much for coming to see our house. Buying a house without a Real Estate Agent is easy and will save you money. To make an offer, simply give us a call with the amount that you would like to offer. Once we come to an agreement, our Real Estate Attorney will send you a sales contract to sign. You will sign the contract, include the deposit of $1,000 and return it to the attorney. We will then sign the contract and provide a copy back to you. Then you can contact your mortgage company, provide them a copy of the signed contract and they will do the rest. Your mortgage company and our Real Estate Attorney/Title Agent will walk you through the entire process step-by-step.*
  - o Include a copy of the appraisal, house inspection, utility bills, warranty, etc.
- ☐ Ask for feedback about the house at the end of the showing:
  - o What was your overall impression of the house?
  - o What did you like most about the house?
  - o Is there anything you wish was different about the house?

CHAPTER 13:
NEGOTIATING THE SALE OF YOUR HOME

Negotiating can be very fun or not so fun. Most of this depends on your own personal feelings. Either way, follow these simple tips to ensure you maximize your outcome.

Before the Offer

☐ Know the lowest price you will accept.

☐ Know the price for which your house is listed. When you are listed on multiple websites, make sure all of them reflect the same price.

☐ Understand what is important to you. Is it getting the most money from your house, having plenty of time to move out, closing on your new house before or after you close on your existing house, not closing on a certain date, etc.?

Once You Receive an Offer

☐ Be polite and thank the buyer for the offer. Even if the offer is ridiculously low, the buyer is interested in your house and you may be able to come to an agreement.

☐ Do not respond immediately; always call back...unless they are offering full price or more.

☐ Repeat the offer back to the buyer/agent.

☐ Discuss the offer with your spouse or partner. Even if your spouse told you to make the deal, your spouse should be part of the process to eliminate any misunderstandings or arguments down the road.

☐ Call your Real Estate Attorney and let him/her know that you are negotiating an offer. Find out:

 o What details are needed to write up the sales contract
 o What the turnaround time will be on the contract
 o How will the contract get to the buyer and then to you
 o How the deposit will be handled

Don't be surprised if the Real Estate Attorney wants to have you and the buyers sign the contract in his/her office. If there are any misunderstandings, you can clear them up right there and still get the contract signed. This is a huge benefit to you!

Counter Offers

- ☐ You will get more money if you always make at least one counter offer, unless you get full asking price and only have one offer.
- ☐ Never reject an offer. Always counter offer and let the buyer walk away. If you reach the lowest amount you would accept, let the buyer know that this is as low as you can go.
- ☐ Always respond to offers promptly. You don't want the buyer to have second thoughts and withdraw the offer. (I once made a counter offer on a Friday to a seller and then rescinded it on Sunday because I had not heard back from the seller and I started doubting my offer.)
- ☐ Once you get into your price range, accept the offer. You should not risk losing an offer because the buyer reached their maximum limit and you just want a little more.

Closing The Deal

- ☐ Get the following information from the seller for the sales contract:
 o First and Last Name of Everyone who is buying the house (Usually the wife and husband)
 o Mailing address
 o Email address
 o Phone number
 o Desired closing date (this can easily be changed in the future)
 o The negotiated amount
 o The bank they will use for the mortgage
 o Any special items, such as concessions to pay for upgrades, repairs, closing costs etc.

- ☐ Tell the buyer what to expect next. Let them know they will receive the sales contract in __ days (no more than 2) and they will need to sign it and send it to your (attorney or Title Agent) along with the deposit of $_____.

- ☐ Keep the deposit amount low. Most sales agreements give ample room to cancel a contract for legitimate reasons and you will rarely be able to keep the deposit if the buyer backs out. You don't want a large deposit to dissuade someone from signing the sales agreement once you have agreed upon a price.

- ☐ Once the deal is finalized, call your Real Estate Attorney and give the details of the offer. Make sure you have all the questions answered on the form provided to you by the attorney.

- ☐ Your Real Estate Attorney will make sure the buyer receives the disclosers.

- ☐ The Attorney should call you once she/he has the signed agreement in hand so you can countersign it.

- ☐ They buyer will deliver the signed contract to their mortgage company and that will get the ball rolling.

Bonus

You can practice negotiating before you even list your house for sale. Try out our Negotiation Simulator at www.fsboacademy.com/freebookbonus.

CHAPTER 14
BETWEEN THE OFFER AND CLOSING

Once you accept an offer, your work is almost complete. But, there are still a few things that need to happen.

> **Bonus**
>
> To better understand how the closing works, check out a free video at www.fsboacademy.com/freebookbonus

Ways to Reduce Stress Before The Closing

- ☐ **Expect some bumps in the road**. As many closings as these professionals do, you would expect everything to run smoothly, but it does not. Know that things will get overlooked, people will miss deadlines, and you will get frustrated. This is all part of the process, so take a deep breath and focus on the house you are going to buy next.
- ☐ **Expect your closing day to be moved several times.** I've only had one closing date that was on time. It just so happened the original closing date was already on the last day of the month so no one wanted to move it to the next month, which would have affected their goals and bonuses.
- ☐ **You are going to get visitors.** If the buyer is taking out a mortgage to buy your house, then all kinds of people are going to visit your house. Expect visits from home inspectors, appraisers, surveyors, contractors,

insurance agents, and the buyers themselves. Most will make appointments and many are good at keeping those appointments, but don't be surprised if they don't. Just reschedule and know that this will all be over soon.

☐ **You will be surprised by the little things found in the Home Inspection.** The home inspector works for the buyer and it is their job to find every little thing that is wrong with your house. My last inspection pointed out some worn insulation that leads to the air conditioner. The report stated concerns for the pipes freezing in the winter...I live in Florida. It does not mean that you have to fix all of these items - the buyer will decide that. A good Real Estate Attorney will protect you by including in the contract a maximum amount you will to pay to have items fixed.

What You Should Do Before The Closing

☐ **Expect Visits from the following:**
   o **House Inspectors** will need access to your house for 2-4 hours. Some buyers will also hire specialized inspectors such as a pool inspector or roof inspector.
   o **Insurance Agents** may need access to your house for 30 minutes. A good insurance agent will visit the house to make key decisions on the policy that is written.
   o **Surveyors** will not need access to the house but will be on your property for up to 2 hours. These are the folks that take measurements and draw up maps of your property. You can take the flags out of the ground after about a week.
   o **Appraisers** will need access to your house for up to 2 hours. A good appraiser will be almost as thorough as a house inspector, but these are few and far between.
   o **The buyer** will want access to your house on several occasions. The more excited the buyer is, the more access he/she will want. Make sure that if you are not there, the buyer's agent is there.

☐ **Set Appointments Promptly**
   o When each of the above individuals call you, return their call promptly and set the appointments as soon as possible. You don't want your lack of availability to result in delaying the closing and paying another mortgage payment.

☐ **Pay your bills on time (mortgage, HOA fees, etc.).** You don't want a lien put on your house at the last minute causing a delay in the closing. Even if a bill is due right after closing, pay it ahead of time and get a refund later.

☐ **Notify your insurance agent of the pending sale.** Note that you may be required to take out extra insurance if you are not going to be residing on the property during the closing.

☐ **Be nice to the buyer.** The buyer may be a big old Pain in the Arse, but be nice. Why? There are about a million and one reasons the buyer can use to back out of the contract. There are also tactics they can use to delay the closing. Be nice and avoid all of this aggravation.

☐ **Check in with everyone weekly.** Call your Attorney, the Title Agent, and the buyer (or the agent) to check in. Just ask, "Is everything still on track for closing on (Date)?" During the last three days of the closing, call everyone daily.

CHAPTER 15
THE DAY OF CLOSING

Congratulations, you made it. Just make sure the last few items are finished and you can close this chapter in your life. (Note that you can do some of this ahead of time if you already moved out.)

☐ Call the closing office one last time to ensure everything is on track. It is normal for closings to come down to the wire.

☐ Take one set of keys to the closing and leave the remainder in the house.

☐ Lower all the shades.

☐ Turn the sprinkler system off.

☐ Change the garage code and leave a note with the new one.

☐ Leave the garage door remotes on the counter.

☐ Leave the appliance manuals on the counter.

☐ Call the utility company and shut off the electricity.

☐ Call the water company and shut off the water.

☐ Cancel the lawn service.

☐ Cancel the garbage service (unless it is a city/county provided service).

☐ Cancel any gas or heating oil services.

☐ Transfer the newspaper to the new house.

☐ Cancel your homeowners insurance.

☐ Transfer the cable/satellite/internet/phone to your new residence.

☐ Call your bank and credit card companies to update your address.

☐ File a change of address with the post office.

☐ Make sure to take your driver's license or state ID to the closing.

☐ Celebrate when the money is deposited to your account!

THE FLUFF IS AT THE END OF THE BOOK

Who Is This Guide For?

This book is not for everyone. Is it for you? Read on...

- If you are scared to sell your house on your own, this book is not for you.
- If you have a lot of questions about how to sell your house on your own, this book is not for you.
- If you are trying to decide whether or not to sell your house on your own, this book is not for you.
- If you live in the urban center of a major metropolitan area, this book is not for you. I have not interviewed any sellers from these areas and am not an expert here. There may be some very significant differences in the way you need to sell your house in these urban centers of which I am not aware.
- If you live in a condo, apartment, boat, or other multifamily non-land based dwelling, this book is not for you. For the same reasons as the urban dwellers, this is not my area of expertise.
- If you live on your own island, this book is not for you.

However, there is a select group of people out there who will benefit from this book.
- Someone who has sold a house on their own before and wants to make sure they are covering all of their bases this time around.
- Someone selling their house on their own for the first time, has done a some research, and just needs a reference guide to help them through the process.

- Someone who lives in a single family house in a suburban area, small town or rural area.

If you purchase this book and decide it is not for you, please return it for a refund. If you are unable to get a refund from the place where you purchased the book, you may contact me directly. Just send a copy of your receipt to jake@fsboacademy.com and I will arrange a refund for you.

If you have found this book to be useful and want to share it with a friend, don't feel bad about doing so. Of course, I would love for your friend to buy the book, but my true desire is to ensure more people sell their house on their own without an agent. So, go for it and thanks for sharing. You can also donate it to your local library when you are finished.

How To Use This Guide

This book is designed to be used as a reference. I encourage you to give it a quick once through and then put it down and return to it during each stage of the house selling process.

When you come to each stage in the house selling process, pick up the book and read that section carefully to ensure you are not missing any part of the process.

Attention: If you have not already hired a Real Estate Attorney, please do so immediately. This will be the best money you spend on your house sale. Go to the section on Hiring a Real Estate Attorney and follow the steps laid out there. This is very important because laws differ state by state and can change every year. A Real Estate Attorney will help protect you.

ABOUT THE AUTHOR

I, Jake Posey, am the founder of FSBO Academy, an organization that helps homeowners sell their home without a real estate agent. FSBO Academy is the first professional website dedicated to teaching homeowners a step-by-step process for selling their home on their own. Students receive a plan to follow and are taught in detail how to execute each part of the plan.

FSBO Academy was founded when I started researching how to sell my first house on my own. I found two types of articles during this research. The first type of article was written by Real Estate Agents "teaching" you how to sell your house on your own and then scaring the hell out of you if you tried it on your own. The second type of article was offered by websites selling MLS listings. These articles were a "mile wide and an inch deep." They told you what you needed to do, but not how to do it.

In the end, I got scared and hired an agent to sell my house. However, after my house sold I saw how easy the process was. This prompted me to interview homeowners who were selling their home without an agent. I put that knowledge to work by helping my mother sell her house on her own.

After more than 50 interviews of successful FSBO homeowners and industry professionals, I decided to start the academy to share what I had learned. Selling your home on your own is super easy!!!

HOW TO GET FREE ACCESS TO THE HOME SELLING ACADEMY

Are you ready to supercharge your learning and get every one of your questions answered? I spent more than 270 hours putting together a 49 video course and a ton of templates to help you kick the agent to the curb.

To access the course, follow these easy steps:

1.   Sign   up   for   your   free   book   bonus   at www.fsboacademy.com/freebookbonus.
2.   Once you have access to the free book bonus, you will see an invitation for you to access the Home Selling Academy. Click on the invitation.
3. Setup a username and password to get immediate access.

HERE IS WHAT YOU'LL GET IN THE HOME SELLING ACADEMY

Lesson 1 - Start Here: Learn the exact steps you need to take to sell your home for top dollar. Find out what extra work you will have to do and how much time it will take you.

Lesson 2 - Get Your Home Ready: Learn how to make your home look great…even on a budget.

Lesson 3 - Put Your Team Together: Learn who does what, who you need to hire and why. Get scripts and worksheets to help you find and hire the right people that will save you time and money.

Lesson 4 - Pricing Your Home: What is the best way to price your home for sale? There are a few that are good and some that are bad. Save thousands of dollars by selecting the right way to price your home for sale. I give you scientifically proven tips to help you get more money for your home by just changing a few numbers in the price.

Lesson 5 - Listing Your Home: Where do you list your home online? Do you have to list it on all the sites? Get answers to these questions and learn exactly how to write your listing description with our easy to follow template. Learn how to take amazing pictures of your home…using your phone.

Lesson 6 - Marketing Your Home: Once you list your home online, you are 80% of the way there. We will teach you advanced methods to get the word out … without ever talking to anyone.

Lesson 7 - Showing Your Home: Learn how to show your home the right way…yes there is a right way. Learn how to show it if the buyer has an agent or if they don't have an agent. Find out how to make your home shine for the showing. Easy forms let you get inside the buyer's head to know just what they are thinking.

Lesson 8 - Open Houses: Should you conduct an open house? Probably not, but take our quiz to find out. If you do, you will get our open house blueprint that will make jaws drop.

Lesson 9 - Negotiating Your Offer: Learn how to make negotiating easy and fun. Get comfortable with the process using our negotiation simulator tool. Find out how to handle different types of offers and become a master negotiator.

Lesson 10 - The Closing: Learn exactly what happens at closing and how you can master this simple process. Find out how to reduce stress and how to save a deal that is falling apart.

What are you waiting for, get your access now: www.fsboacademy.com/freebookbonus

Made in the USA
Middletown, DE
03 May 2018